THE STORY
A Season

Written by Carol Ann Morrow
Illustrated by Miguel D. Lopez
ISBN 1-936020-19-5

Artwork and Text © 2011 Aquinas Kids, Phoenix, Arizona.

Lent is the Church's springtime. We use this season to grow, just as the flowers begin to bud and the world turns green again. The cross reminds us of what Jesus did for us.

During Lent, Catholics and other Christians choose to do things that will help them become better followers of Jesus. These are called penances. Draw a picture of what this boy (and you) might choose to do for Lent.

The color of Lent is purple (violet). In the Church, it is considered the color of penance and sorrow. Your priest will wear a purple vestment at Mass. Where can you use the color purple here?

The 40 days of Lent are like the days that Moses spent on Mount Sinai preparing to receive the Ten Commandments for his people.

The 40 days of Lent are also like the days that Jesus spent in the desert preparing for his public mission. We have a mission too.

The Church encourages us to do three things during Lent. Prayer, speaking and listening to God, is first.

Good works, or acts of kindness, is the second important Lenten activity.

Fasting is the third Lenten practice. For adults between 18 and 59, this is about how much they eat and when. For people your age, it may be a choice to eat more vegetables and less dessert. You can decide.

On Ash Wednesday, we receive the Sign of the Cross on our forehead. When the ashes are blessed, the priest prays, "Lord, bless these ashes by which we show that we are dust."

True penance is making choices that turn us toward God—not to show off for people to see.

Jesus told his disciples what behaviors he wanted of them and how he would judge them at the end of time. First, he said, "For I was hungry and you gave me to eat."

"I was thirsty and you gave me drink."

"I was a stranger and you welcomed me."

"I was naked and you clothed me."

"I was ill and you cared for me."

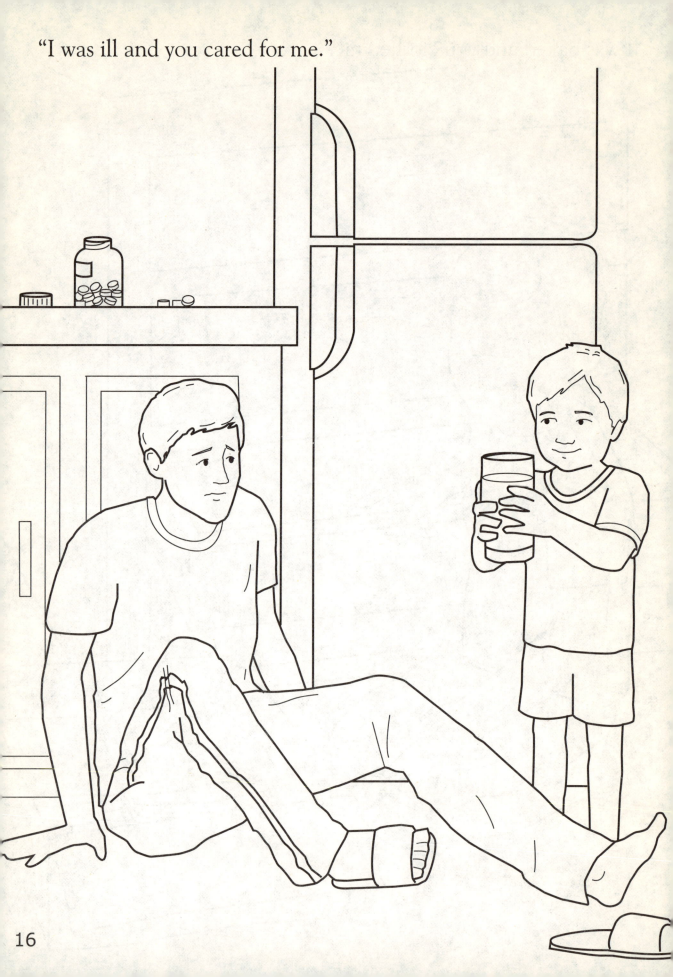

"I was in prison and you visited me."

Jesus also told his disciples, "Do unto others as you would have others do unto you." We call this the Golden Rule. It is good to practice this rule, especially during Lent.

Jesus told his disciples, "Love your enemies." We are his disciples too. It is easy to love those who love you, but to be kind to those who don't is the real test of a follower of Jesus.

Jesus also says that forgiveness and generosity are the marks of his disciples. He says that when you give, you will receive even more, so much that you can hardly hold it all.

The Fourth Sunday of Lent is sometimes called Laetare Sunday. Laetare means rejoice. We are happy because we are now halfway through Lent. The priest may choose to wear a rose-colored vestment instead of the usual Lenten purple. Use your rose—or pink—color for his vestment.

On Palm Sunday, Jesus rode into Jerusalem followed by many who believed in him. They shouted "Hosanna" and waved palm branches in his honor.

The last Wednesday of Lent is sometimes called Spy Wednesday. We remember that the apostle Judas Iscariot told those who feared and hated Jesus that he would show them where to find Jesus and arrest him.

On Holy Thursday morning, your bishop or archbishop celebrates Mass with the priests of your area. He does this in imitation of Jesus who celebrated the first Mass with his apostles on this day.

On Holy Thursday, the priests renew their promise to be good followers of the Apostles. They then pray for their Bishop that he will do the same.

On Holy Thursday evening, the priests will wash the feet of 12 members of the parish just as Jesus washed the feet of his disciples at the Last Supper.

After Mass on Holy Thursday, the Blessed Sacrament is taken to a special place and the altar is stripped bare. This reminds us of Jesus asking his apostles to pray with him the night before he was arrested.

On Good Friday we remember that Jesus gave up his life for us on the Cross.

On Good Friday during the afternoon Communion service, the cross is given special honor (called veneration). We pray, "This is the wood of the Cross, on which hung the Savior of the world. Come let us worship."

On Holy Saturday evening at the Easter vigil, the Easter fire is blessed. Good Friday was a day of darkness. Now we are ready to welcome the light of Christ.

A large candle is lit from this new fire. It is a symbol of Jesus risen from the dead. We pray, "May the Light of Christ, rising in glory, remove the darkness of our hearts and minds."

Everyone in the church may light a small candle from the light which stands for Christ. As the priest carries the candle toward the front of church and the light grows and grows, we pray, "Christ our Light. Thanks be to God." This is what we celebrate on Easter.